Poverty is a growing problem in this rich country. More and more people are homeless. Many people cannot take care of their children. Even people with jobs are struggling to make a living. Most Americans agree that more should be done to help the poor. But what?

This country spends a lot of money on welfare programs. But they are not working very well. The problem is getting worse. Most people think that the welfare system should be changed or replaced. But they do not agree on how this should be done.

We need to talk about what our choices are. The National Issues Forums (NIF) give people a way to meet and talk with others about important issues. They also give people a way to share their views with the nation's leaders.

Each year, three important topics are chosen for discussion. Issue books are written for each topic. Each book gives different ideas on how we might attack the problem. The books present several plans for action on the issue. People read the books. Then they meet with others in Forums. Each year, NIF reports results of the Forums to local and national leaders.

Talking together about issues is important to our democracy. When you join in, you hear the views of others. You compare their ideas with your own views and values. You take part, both as an individual and as a member of your community.

Your views can be heard by our leaders. You will find two ballots at the back of this book. Please fill one out before you read the book or go to a Forum. Fill out the other ballot after the Forum. It is important to fill out both ballots and return them to NIF.

Every American's thoughts and feelings are important. NIF invites you to join in the talk and be heard.

Ilse Tebbetts

Ilse Tebbetts
Managing Editor

Managing Editor: Ilse Tebbetts
Writer: Ilse Tebbetts
Copy Editor: Betty Frecker
Research: Bill Carr
Ballots: Randa Slim, Steve Farkas,
        John Doble, Ilse Tebbetts
Design and Production: George Cavanaugh

Circulation Coordinator:
    Victoria Simpson
Cover Illustration: David Gothard
Formatting: UTC Communications Group
Graphic Research: Bill Carr
Production Director: Robert E. Daley

The books in this series are adapted from materials written by Keith Melville and Bill Carr of the Public Agenda Foundation — a nonprofit, nonpartisan organization devoted to research and education about public issues — and by the Kettering Foundation. The Kendall/Hunt Publishing Company prints and distributes these books. They are used by civic and educational organizations interested in addressing public issues.

In particular, they are used in local discussion groups that are part of a nationwide network, the National Issues Forums (NIF). The NIF consists of thousands of educational organizations — colleges and universities, libraries, service clubs, and membership groups. Although each community group is locally controlled, NIF is a collaborative effort. Each year, convenors choose three issues and use common materials — issue books such as this one, and parallel audio and videotape materials.

The abridged editions are designed to expand the audience to include both adult and young new readers. The material has been rewritten at a level appropriate to these groups, and reviewed by the Pennsylvania State University Institute for the Study of Adult Literacy.

Groups interested in using the NIF materials and adapting its approach as part of their own program are invited to write or call for further information: National Issues Forums, 100 Commons Road, Dayton, Ohio 45459-2777. Phone 1-800-433-7834.

The NIF issue books — both the standard edition and the abridged version at a lower reading level, as well as audiocassette and videocassette versions of the same material — can be ordered from Kendall/Hunt Publishing Company, 2460 Kerper Boulevard, Dubuque, Iowa 52004-0539. Phone 1-800-228-0810. The following titles are available:

The Poverty Puzzle: What Should Be Done to Help the Poor?
Prescription for Prosperity: Four Paths to Economic Renewal
Criminal Violence: What Direction Now for the War on Crime?
The Health Care Crisis: Containing Costs, Expanding Coverage
The Boundaries of Free Speech: How Free Is Too Free?
America's Role in the World: New Risks, New Realities
Energy Options: Finding a Solution to the Power Predicament
The Battle over Abortion: Seeking Common Ground in a Divided Nation
Regaining the Competitive Edge: Are We Up to the Job?
Remedies for Racial Inequality: Why Progress Has Stalled, What Should Be Done
The Day Care Dilemma: Who Should Be Responsible for the Children?
The Drug Crisis: Public Strategies for Breaking the Habit
The Environment at Risk: Responding to Growing Dangers
Health Care for the Elderly: Moral Dilemmas, Mortal Choices
Coping with AIDS: The Public Response to the Epidemic

The Poverty Puzzle: What Should Be Done to Help the Poor?

Contents

Introduction:
Rethinking Poverty

In the 1960s, President Lyndon Johnson started a War on Poverty. Today, we seem to be losing that war. More and more Americans are becoming poor. We need to look at better ways to help them.

America is one of the richest countries in the world. But more than 35 million Americans are poor. That includes one out of every five American children. We have the highest rate of child poverty of any industrial country.

Polls show that most Americans are concerned about the poor. They feel sorry for people who have run into bad luck. But polls also show that many Americans resent the welfare system. They believe the system is a mess. They think it keeps poor people from helping themselves. They believe many poor people cheat and lie to get welfare.

In the 1960s, the economy of this country was growing. Most people were making a good living. They were more willing to spend tax money to help the poor.

Today, many people are having a hard time making a living. They are not as willing to pay taxes to help the poor. They are more concerned with what the poor should do to help themselves.

Basic changes in our system of aid to the poor have been proposed. One huge program is Aid to Families with Dependent Children. This is called AFDC. During the 1992 election, President Clinton proposed a time limit on AFDC: no one would get AFDC for more than two years. Other proposals also put limits on cash payments made to the poor.

Some call for providing minimum wage jobs when payments end.

Congress is looking at many proposals. But any changes will affect millions of Americans. So we **all** need to think about this issue. We need to look at the whole problem. Why are so many Americans poor? What do we owe our fellow Americans? What kinds of programs are likely to help the poor help themselves?

How It Was

In 1932, Franklin Roosevelt was elected president. It was the time of the Great Depression. Banks failed. People lost their jobs. Farms blew away in dust storms. Many Americans became poor. President Roosevelt was deeply concerned about "one-third of a nation ill-fed, ill-clad, and ill-housed."

One result was the Social Security Act, passed in 1935. It provided an old-age pension. It also provided unemployment insurance for people who lost their jobs. And it set up AFDC. This program provides payments for women with children whose fathers do not support them.

Before that time, the federal government did not much concern itself with the poor. If family

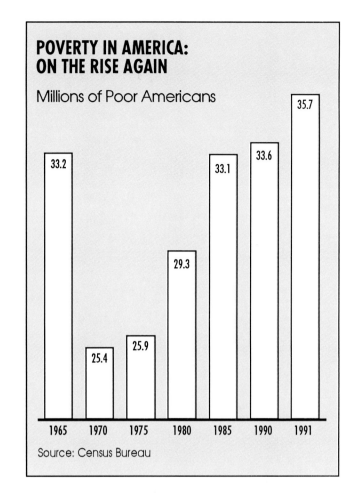

POVERTY IN AMERICA: ON THE RISE AGAIN

Millions of Poor Americans

Year	Millions
1965	33.2
1970	25.4
1975	25.9
1980	29.3
1985	33.1
1990	33.6
1991	35.7

Source: Census Bureau

members or charities did not help, you were out of luck. The Social Security Act changed that whole way of thinking. It gave the federal government a new role. The government now protected people against some of life's hardships. It provided money to the needy.

Who Are America's Poor?

ARLENE GOTTFRIED

- In 1992, a family of four was poor if its income was less than $14,463.

- Single people were poor if their income was less than $7,202.

- In 1991, one out of every seven Americans was poor. That was 35.7 million people.

- Over 14 million children were poor in 1991.

- About 40% of the poor live in families where someone works at least part-time.

In the 1960s, President Johnson declared a War on Poverty. The government would still help. But its focus would be different. It would help people lift **themselves** out of poverty. The goal was to give people "a hand, not a handout." Job training programs were started. Loan programs helped students get through school.

Other aid programs were also started or expanded in the 1960s. Medicaid was created in 1965 to provide health care for the poor. Food Stamp and public housing programs were expanded.

Many people thought that we could win the war against poverty. But by the 1970s it became clear that the system was not working. Things were not getting better for poor people in this country. They were getting worse. And aid programs were costing more and more money.

What Now?

States share costs of some aid programs with the federal government. Many states are having money problems. They are finding it harder and harder to balance their budgets. In 1991 and 1992, dozens of states reduced benefits to the poor.

Some states have made new rules. For example, New Jersey now limits benefits to AFDC mothers. If a mother has **another** child, she cannot collect more benefits. Some states are thinking of other changes in AFDC rules. These would encourage women to stay in school or get married. Or, they would make people work if they are able.

This raises new questions. What do the poor owe in return for their benefits? Should they have to do certain things to get public support? What happens to them if they don't? What happens to their children?

Deciding how to fix the system will not be easy. We will have to make hard choices between different things we believe in:

- We want to help people who need help. But we also want to encourage people to help themselves.

- We feel we should help people who are not working. But we do not want to encourage people to quit low-wage jobs to get welfare.

- We want to support needy single-parent families. But we do not want to encourage more single-parent families.

In this book, we focus on four approaches to the problem.

Choice #1 blames the problem on too much government help. In this view, public handouts have discouraged people from getting jobs. This has undermined family life. We should cut back — or cut out — public payments to the poor.

Choice #2 says the government has done too **little** for the poor. Poverty should not be blamed on the poor. The fault lies with our economic system. We owe the poor a decent living.

Choice #3 agrees that the poor deserve help. The problem arises when they are not required to do anything in exchange. In return for getting public aid, they should work if they can. They should stop having children they cannot support. They should finish high school.

Choice #4 sees the lack of jobs as the basic problem. Millions of Americans cannot find a way to make a decent living. We should make every effort to create more jobs. And we should ensure that those who do work are not poor.

Each of these choices is based on a different view of what causes poverty. Each suggests a different course of action. Some people favor combining more than one of these ideas. We need to talk about all of them. We need to take a fresh look at what should be done about poverty in this country. This is what we will be doing in these Forums.

MODELL/ THE NEW YORKER

Time to Get Back on My Feet

Tasha Barber, 20, is a second-generation welfare mom. She dropped out of her Bronx high school after her first son was born four years ago. A second son, by a different father, came along last year. . . . She had a minimum wage job in a supermarket for about a year, she says, "but they weren't paying enough so I quit and went on welfare." Her 2-bedroom Harlem apartment costs $238.50 a month, which is paid directly by the government. In addition, she receives $190.50 in AFDC and $219 in food stamps. . . . Last January, Barber began attending vocational-training classes at the National Puerto Rican Forum in the South Bronx. She is looking for work through the forum's placement service. "It's time for me to get back on my feet," Barber declares. "I want a job because I want my kids to have what I didn't."

Reprinted with permission
Time magazine, May 25, 1992

I Never Had to Take Money Before

Sean Hanan never expected to be on welfare. But bad luck — and the recession — caught up with him. After graduating from high school . . . he worked part-time at a Sears distribution center. When his hours were cut back, he moved to Iowa in search of work but could find nothing. By that time, married with two young daughters, Hanan, now 24, had no choice but to go on the dole. "I never had to take money before," he says. The family received $495 a month through Iowa's Aid to Families with Dependent Children-Unemployed Parent program, as well as $229 in food stamps. "People who used to live in the middle class now live in the lower class," he says, gazing at the battered furniture and empty pantry of his rented two-bedroom apartment. "Two cars, nice houses — that goal is just unattainable."

Reprinted with permission
Time magazine, May 25, 1992

8

Choice # 1:
The Welfare Trap

Spending more money on aid to the poor is not the answer. Welfare programs have been a large part of the problem. They have made people depend too much on the government instead of helping themselves.

In 1992, Vice President Dan Quayle made a speech in New York City. He talked about the city's problems. He pointed out that one in four New Yorkers was poor. This was the highest level of poverty in ten years.

The vice president blamed the problem on the "welfare state." Others who share this view agree. They say that the chief cause of America's poverty is not too **little** public spending on welfare. It is too **much.** Welfare is supposed to help the poor. Instead, it has created more poverty by making people depend on public handouts.

Those who favor Choice #1 see the hard facts like this: Since 1970, $3.7 **trillion** has been spent to help the poor. What is the result? In 1970, 12.6% of Americans were poor. By 1991, 14.2% of Americans were poor. And, the number is going up.

Charles Murray wrote a book called *Losing Ground.* He put it this way: "We tried to provide more for the poor and produced more poor instead." We tried to help people escape from poverty, he said. Instead, we "built a trap."

The Trap

Since the 1960s, more and more money has been spent to relieve poverty. Why then has the poverty problem gotten worse? In this view, the

problem is the welfare system itself. Giving people money because they are poor rewards poverty. It makes it possible for poor people to live without working. And so, poverty goes on and on.

Charles Murray says that in the 1970s, benefits increased faster than wages. He says people were tempted to take the easy way. They did not ask what they could do for themselves. They asked what the government could do for them.

People who agree with Choice #1 worry about two things:

1. The welfare system rewards poor people for not working.

2. The welfare system undermines the family.

Say you are a single mother of two children and have no job. In 1992, in New York City, you could get a monthly AFDC check for $577. You could get $229 worth of food stamps. You could get $286 toward your rent. Medicaid would pay for health costs. And you could get help with day care if you went to classes.

But now, say you get a job. It might not pay very much. But the minute you begin earning money your benefits would be reduced. You would get less in food stamps. You would get less help with housing. You may not qualify for Medicaid. And you would have to worry about the costs of day care. You may decide it just does not pay to work.

What effect does the welfare system have on families? There are more and more families headed only by a mother. In the past 25 years the number of these families has almost tripled. In this view, the welfare system must take a lot of the blame.

If fathers choose not to support their children, the government steps in. The mother can get cash payments from AFDC. In most states, an unmarried mother can get more AFDC if she has more children.

The man might choose to marry the woman. He may get work. His job may not pay enough to support the family. But if it is a full-time job, welfare benefits end.

In this view, most low-income men quickly get the message. The best thing they can do for their families is to leave them. A family can get **some** welfare aid when the father is there. But they can do better without him.

Hard Lessons

Those who agree with Choice #1 say that welfare is not good for the poor. They believe that

Welfare Fraud

Officials say many poor people are cheating the welfare system. This is costing American taxpayers billions of dollars a year. Here are some ways people cheat the system:

Filing Fake Claims: You have to prove who you are when you apply for AFDC. Some people show false birth certificates or Social Security cards. In one famous case, a California woman used 12 different names. She collected $377,000 in 8 years. She owned a Rolls Royce car. She lived in a 22-room house.

Working without Telling: This is the most common type of welfare fraud. Poor people get less medical, food, and cash benefits if they earn money. So, many feel it does not pay to be honest about working.

Trading Food Stamps: Food stamps are often used to buy other things. For instance, a man may buy drugs on the street for food stamps. He sells $100 of food stamps for $50 worth of drugs. The drug dealer sells the stamps to a grocery store clerk for $75. The clerk goes to the bank. He turns in the food stamps for their full value. Everyone made money. But no food was bought.

Traveling for Welfare: Some states pay higher AFDC benefits than others. Some welfare cheaters live in one state and collect welfare there. But they also set up fake addresses in other states. Then they travel to these places to collect more AFDC.

---

government should get out of the welfare business. This would be very hard on some people for a while. But, in the long run, it would be better. It would be better for them and for the country.

What would happen if welfare were cut back or cut out? Poor people would have to get help from private charities. They would have to depend on homeless shelters. They would have to get food from soup kitchens.

Living like this would be very tough on some people. But, in this view, it would be kinder in the long run. It would force able-bodied people to look for work. More families would stay together. Without government handouts, they would have to start helping themselves.

What Critics Say

Critics disagree with this choice for different reasons. Some say that those who favor this view do not have their facts straight. For one thing, many

"Otis, shout at that man to pull himself together."

poor people work. They earn some money. So they do not qualify for welfare checks. Many of those who do get welfare, do not **stay** on welfare. So, how can welfare be blamed for their life-style?

Some say that the root of the problem is our economic system. The system provides low wages for many. It provides no jobs at all for millions of others. Welfare programs are not to blame for poverty. Welfare programs have kept the poverty rate from going even **higher**.

Critics say many people have the wrong idea about the poor. When they think of the poor they see this picture: they see an inner-city black woman. She has no husband. She has one baby after another. Her boyfriend sells crack on street corners.

Yet, most of America's poor are not minorities. Most do not live in inner cities. Many of them work. Most of the poor are like the rest of us, critics say. They are having a hard time making a living. They need a little help now and then to get on their feet.

Those who favor Choice #1 sometimes talk about "welfare queens." They mean that some people are living well at public expense. Critics point out that people do not get rich on welfare. In fact, most needy people do not get enough. The average AFDC check to a family of three was $372 a month in 1992. This is far below the poverty level.

Many states are thinking of cutting back on public aid. Some have already done so. It will save money. But critics ask what will happen to people who are cut off. Where will they next be seen, asks newspaper writer Neal Peirce. "In jobs? Or in homeless shelters? Or in police lineups? Or in prison?"

Many critics agree that the poverty issue is not clear. The answers are not easy to find. But they say we must start with one basic idea. A humane society should meet basic living needs of **all** its citizens. We will look at that view next.

STEVEN PUMPHREY

Most of America's poor are not minorities. Most do not live in inner cities. Many of them work.

Choice #2:
The Rights of the Poor

Poor people have a right to public help. They should be able to live decently. They should be able to take care of their children. A society with humane values owes that to all its citizens.

This choice begins with a very different idea about the poor. It begins with the idea that the poor have a **right** to public help.

Almost 50 years ago, a United Nations Commission wrote a Bill of Rights. They wrote it for the people of the world. One part says that everyone has the right to a decent standard of living. That means enough food and clothing. It means decent housing and medical care.

Many people believe in these rights. The National Conference of Catholic Bishops wrote about them in 1986. They wrote a report called *Economic Justice for All.* Our economic system leaves too many people poor, the bishops said. This hurts all of us. The report said that America should ensure basic economic rights for everyone.

Holes in the Safety Net

Acrobats in the circus often have a safety net. This keeps them from crashing to the ground if they fall. Choice #2 is concerned with a safety net for the poor.

Many wealthy countries offer income support programs to everyone. These programs work like safety nets. They keep people from falling into poverty. The U.S. system offers very few benefits to everyone. You have to prove you are poor to get most benefits.

NICULAE ASCIU

And, even if you qualify, many programs do not pay enough, in this view. An average poor family may get food stamps and AFDC. Together, these bring their income to only 70% of the poverty level. In some states, like Alabama, they do not even reach 50%.

Many government budgets have been cut in the past few years. Programs that help the middle class have hardly been touched. But the value of benefits to the poor has dropped. Take a poor family of three in a typical state. In 1992, they got much less help than they got in 1970. The value of their benefits dropped by 43%.

Medicaid is another problem. This program was started in 1965. The idea was that everyone should be able to get health care. And nobody would get second-class care. Today, Medicaid falls far short of that goal.

The number of people who qualify for Medicaid went up in the 1980s. But many **are** treated like second-class citizens, those who favor this choice say. This is because Medicaid pays doctors only about half their usual fee. So, many doctors do not want to take Medicaid patients. Poor people are often forced to go from doctor to doctor. They have to beg for health care.

It is clear that the poor are in trouble. But cuts in aid to the poor go on. Those cuts affect single

ANDREA MOHIN/NYT PICTURES

DECLINING BENEFITS

Average combined value of AFDC and food stamp benefits for a parent and two children with no other income. (1991 dollars)

1972	$10,169
1976	$9,473
1980	$8,155
1984	$7,567
1988	$7,676
1991	$7,471

Source: House Ways and Means Committee

mothers and their children most of all. One in five American children is poor. This is not only hard on children. It also means serious long-term costs for our society, in this view. Many of these children will become adults who cannot support themselves. It would cost less to help them now than later.

Beyond Our Control

In this view, many Americans are poor through no fault of their own. The fault is in our free market system. Here are some of the things that have gone wrong:

• The gap between the rich and the poor keeps getting wider. In the 1980s, the rich got richer. Their income went **up** 14%. During the same time, the poor got poorer. Their income went **down** 2%.

• Job loss is higher than ever. About 1.8 million workers lost their jobs between 1990 and 1992. The economy is likely to get better. But many of those jobs are not likely to return.

No Place to Call Home

Here is a common sight on many city streets. It is a ragged man wrapped in a dirty blanket. He is trying to stay warm from a heating vent on the sidewalk. He holds a sign. It says "I am hungry and homeless. Please help."

The number of homeless people in this country is growing. No one knows exactly how many there are. The Urban Institute says there are about 600,000. People who work with the homeless think there are closer to 3 million.

Most are single men between the ages of 30 and 50. They often have bad health problems. They may be drug and alcohol addicts. Many are mentally ill.

Only about 15% of the homeless are children. But children are the fastest growing part of the homeless population.

In the early 1980s, many people were sorry for the homeless. But as their numbers grew, people began to get annoyed. They were tired of seeing dirty homeless people in public places. They did not like being bothered by beggars.

So, many cities have begun making laws against begging and vagrancy. In Santa Barbara, it is now illegal to sleep on a public street. Police in Chicago clear homeless people out of the airport. In Miami, it is against the law to beg from people in stopped cars.

In some cities, courts have upheld the rights of the homeless. In Miami, a judge scolded city officials for "driving the homeless from public places." He said the homeless had certain rights. He ordered the city to create "safe zones." These were places where the homeless could stay without being arrested.

People who work for the homeless are pleased with this ruling. But they are also concerned. It means that the homeless have rights to be in **some** public places. But it also seems to mean something else. If they go into **other** places, they could be arrested. It is still not clear what rights the homeless have.

Please DON'T GIVE TO BEGGARS
They Cause Traffic Problems

STEVE NORTHUP/TIME MAGAZINE

• The poor economy has affected minorities more than others. Many minority workers had factory jobs. Those are the jobs that are least likely to come back.

The problem is not that the poor will not work, say those who favor Choice #2. The problem is that they cannot earn enough to make a living. Public aid programs are a way of making up to them for a sometimes cruel system.

In this view, the War on Poverty did not fail. It is true that poverty is bad today. But it would be much worse without aid programs.

What We Should Do

People who support Choice #2 say we must do more to help the poor.

• We should spend more on programs for

children and young people. This includes more funding for Head Start. We must make it easier for the poor to get day care. **Everyone** should have access to good health care.

• We need stronger job training programs. Rebecca Blank is an expert on jobs and workers. She says that adults who have had job training work more and earn more.

• We should raise the level of direct aid to the needy poor. For example, AFDC and food stamps are not enough. They still leave people way below the poverty level.

We are the richest country in the world. In this view, we have put up with growing poverty for too long. It is time to do what we did in the 1960s. We must give the poor a lot more help.

What Critics Say

Critics take a different view of what we owe the poor. They do not believe more government programs will help. The War on Poverty was supposed to help people help themselves. But that has not really happened, they say. The poor have been given more money. They have been given more help. But these programs have not helped people stand on their own feet.

Public programs are very costly, some critics say. For example, AFDC now costs taxpayers about $25 billion a year. Those who favor Choice #2 say this is not enough. They say a poor family still cannot live decently. But critics do not agree. They say if you count **all** benefits, a careful family could manage.

Some of the poor deserve help, critics say. But what about those who do not deserve help? What about winos and drug addicts? What about bums who could work but choose not to? Why should we have to support people who will not help themselves?

There is another basic problem with poverty programs, some say. We say we want to help people get on their own feet. But, critics say, that does not happen very much. Not many welfare mothers are working. Not many are looking for work.

Some people think the right to public help should be limited. It should be offered only to people who will try to help themselves. We should **require** poor people to do certain things to get public aid. We should require that they go to school or look for work or get job training. We will look at that view next.

Choice #3:
A New Compact with The Poor

Our system for helping the poor should be based on "tough love." Public aid should be offered to the needy. But, in return, the poor would have to behave in certain useful ways.

So far, we have talked about two opposing views. Is the government doing too much for the poor? Or is it doing too little? Choice #3 focuses on a different kind of question: What should the poor be required to do in return for public help?

This choice is about a contract between the government and the poor. The government will provide benefits to help the poor. In exchange, the poor will have to do certain things to help themselves.

President Clinton made this point when he ran for office in 1992. The poor deserve help, he said. And the government should do more to help them. "But, when you can, you **must** work," he said. That is because "welfare should be a second chance, not a way of life."

Why We Lost the War

The War on Poverty was a huge effort to wipe out poverty. Why did it fail? According to Choice #3, the reason is this: these programs put the responsibility for change on society. They did not call on poor people to share that responsibility.

SHELLY KATZ/BLACK STAR

The system provided new benefits to the needy. But, in this view, the system focused on the wrong problem. The problem was not just lack of income. There was another reason these programs failed, according to writer Lawrence Mead. They failed because they ignored the behavior of the poor. They did not tell the poor that they ought to **act** differently.

Most of all, government programs did not encourage the poor to work. In 1959, 67% of poor heads of families worked at least part-time. By 1989, only 49% worked at all. Mead says that is the main reason most of them are poor.

Why are so many able-bodied poor **not** working today? And, what can we do to turn that around? Those are the main questions, say those who favor this choice.

There are many reasons why the poor do not work. They include low wages and not enough jobs. But Mead and others say these reasons do not really explain the problem. There may not be enough well-paying jobs.

But there is plenty of low-paying work. Why do so many of the poor not take these jobs? What is missing is the idea that they ought to work, Mead says. "Work is not something the poor feel they **must** do."

In this view, benefits are given as though they are owed. But too little is expected in return.

The Social Contract

Living together in any society means agreeing on certain rules. It means sharing in certain benefits. It also means following the rules to get those benefits. That is the social contract. It is like a business contract. You agree to do certain things in return for getting things you want.

Most Americans agree about certain things.

• Children should study hard and finish high school.

• Young people should not have children until they can support them.

• Able-bodied adults are expected to work at a steady job.

• Everyone is expected to obey the law.

In this view, the welfare system should require the same things of the poor. Isabel Sawhill is an expert on social policy. She says people who follow these rules are not likely to be poor for long. Sometimes, people follow the rules and are still poor. But then, society is much more likely to help them. Too many people are not fulfilling their end of the bargain. That is the problem today, Sawhill says.

What Should Be Done?

The government now spends a lot on helping the poor. Those who support Choice #3 favor such spending. They think benefits should stay about the same. But they do not believe these benefits should provide a free ride. There should be a contract between taxpayers and the poor. The poor should have to honor that contract. They should have to behave in certain ways to qualify for benefits.

New kinds of aid programs have been tried in many states. These programs have tied benefits to certain kinds of behavior.

Workfare programs **require able-bodied people to work.** In this view, work is the most important requirement. One such program was started in 6 counties in Ohio in 1983. Adults receiving aid had to work in public service jobs such as sweeping streets. They had to work 25 hours a week. Over time, fewer people were on AFDC in these counties.

Most Americans agree that a citizen has both rights and duties. And the first duty is to work for a living. A poll was taken in May 1992. It showed that 87% favor welfare rules that require work.

Learnfare is the name of a plan for **encouraging people to stay in school.** A high school education is one of the best ways to avoid poverty. Learnfare programs have been tried in Ohio and Wisconsin. A learnfare program was proposed by the governor of California. It was for teenage mothers on AFDC. If they stayed in school they would get another $50 a month. If they dropped out, they would get $50 less.

Many parents have babies they cannot support.

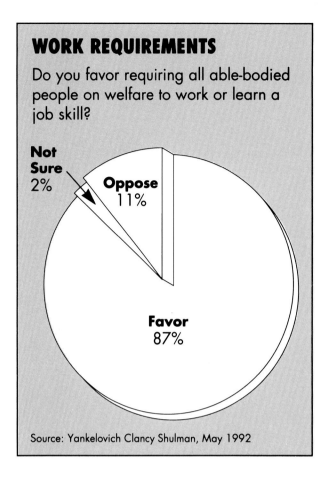

WORK REQUIREMENTS

Do you favor requiring all able-bodied people on welfare to work or learn a job skill?

Not Sure 2%

Oppose 11%

Favor 87%

Source: Yankelovich Clancy Shulman, May 1992

This keeps more families in poverty. It also raises welfare costs. Some states are trying to change rules for AFDC payments. Such plans would **cut off AFDC benefits for added children.**

Ellen Goodman is a writer. She says, "A family that works does not get a raise for having a child. Why should a family that doesn't work?" Working families have to think about whether they can afford another child. "Why not AFDC mothers?" Goodman asks.

Offering poor people bonuses for using birth control has also been proposed. One such plan was proposed in Kansas in 1992. It would have paid AFDC mothers $500 to use Norplant. This is a birth control drug implanted in the woman's arm. But this proposal outraged many people. They thought the state should not try to control a woman's body. The plan was turned down.

Some AFDC mothers get off welfare by getting a job. But even more get off welfare by

NICULAE ASCIU

marrying. Some states are thinking of a plan called "wedfare." This would encourage AFDC mothers to marry and leave AFDC. In Wisconsin, supporters favor offering a $2,000 bonus to women who do this.

In this view, the system must be both kind and fair. America's poor have a right to help from society. But the poor must do their share as well. That is only fair.

What Critics Say

Many Choice #3 ideas seem to make a lot of sense. They seem to be fair. And yet, there are many critics of this approach. They say it will not work. And they say it meddles too much in people's private lives.

Workfare fails for many reasons, critics say. For one thing, many people on welfare are not **able** to work. Some are mentally ill. Others cannot read or write. Also, few jobs for low-skill workers pay enough to live on. They do not lead to better jobs. Workfare and learnfare programs sound good, say critics. But there is not much evidence that they succeed.

Some who favor Choice #3 think poor people have too many children. But most AFDC mothers only have one or two children, critics point out. They have fewer children, on average, than most American families. Cutting benefits for added children will not help much, critics say. Worse, it would punish children for their mothers' behavior. It would push children even farther into poverty.

Choice #3 calls for forcing people to change their behavior to get public aid. It means government would have to find out a lot about what people do. Many Americans do not like this idea. They do not want government meddling so much in people's private lives.

Some critics point out that 40% of poor adults work. About 10% work full-time and are **still** poor. There are more and more working Americans who are poor. They are not poor because they will not work.

The real problem is not the behavior of the poor, these critics say. The real problem is lack of decent jobs. We should not try to mix work and welfare. What we have to do is fix the job market. We will look at that approach in the next section.

Choice #4: Jobs Strategy

> The problem is not our society's values. It is not how the poor behave. The problem is a lack of jobs. This country does not have enough jobs to keep millions of Americans above the poverty line.

The first three choices are concerned with public aid. Choice #4 is concerned with jobs. People who support this choice do not want to improve welfare programs. They want to **replace** those programs with jobs programs.

This approach begins with the idea that everyone who **can** work **should** work. But society has a responsibility, too. It is not to give people money. It is to provide a job for everyone who needs one. It is to make sure the job pays enough to live on. Americans should all have a chance to make it on their own.

Out of Work

Recent polls show that most people agree. They believe that government should ensure jobs for everyone. But we are not even close to meeting that goal. And we are moving farther from it every day. In 1991 and 1992, the jobless rate was around 7%. That was the highest it had been in ten years. It meant more than nine million Americans were out of work.

The official jobless rate is not even the whole story. It does not count people who have given up looking for work. It does not count part-time workers looking for full-time work. If all these people are counted, the jobless rate would be much higher. The **real** rate could be more than 13%.

In this view, lack of jobs explains a lot of what is wrong in America today. Take the Los Angeles riots, for example. Choice #4 argues that a severe lack of jobs was one cause of the riots. The jobless rate was 4.6 % in Los Angeles in June 1990. Then many defense plants laid off workers or closed. Unemployment jumped to 10% just two years later. That was when the riots happened.

Lack of jobs has hit minority workers hard. It affects minority young people **especially** hard. The riots took place in an area of Los Angeles called Watts-Willowbrook. Almost 80,000 jobless young

DAVID GOTHARD

people live there. Nationwide, almost 40% of black teenagers cannot find jobs.

The basic problem is this, says writer William Greider, "Too many workers are chasing too few jobs."

Jobs were a big issue in the 1992 election. All three candidates for president agreed that creating new jobs is important. But in this view, one thing has still not been made clear. The job problem is the main cause of the poverty problem. To wipe out poverty, we must deal with the jobs problem.

The Working Poor

Low wages are another problem, say those who favor this choice. The poor are not all unemployed. Two-thirds of America's poor families include at least one worker. Most are employed part-time. Some work full-time but only for part of the year. Many of these people are women raising their

children alone. They cannot earn enough money to make a decent living.

About 2 million poor Americans work full-time all year. Still they cannot lift themselves above the poverty level. These are the working poor. In 1979, 12% of full-time workers were poor. By 1992, this number had gone up to 20%.

These people are doing what society expects. They are working. They often put in long hours at hard jobs. But they are not getting ahead. They are not paid much. Most have no health benefits. They have no chance to move up. Worst of all, they cannot count on their jobs. When the economy slows down, their jobs are the first to go. They have little or no savings. So they are often just one paycheck away from welfare.

Jobs Programs

We need a healthy economy to provide decent-paying jobs. Those who favor this choice say private businesses are our best hope. They would be the best source of good jobs in the long run. But we must face facts. There are not enough private jobs for all the unemployed.

Coretta Scott King says "The private sector cannot do it all." She says we need job programs funded by the government.

Senators David Boren and Paul Simon have proposed a jobs program. This program would create many public service jobs. Much work needs to be done across the nation. Work such as repairing sidewalks or fixing up parks is needed everywhere. The Boren-Simon plan would provide funds to pay for that work. The work would be for anyone who is unemployed. It would pay minimum wages. This plan would leave public aid programs in place. It would encourage people to work at public service jobs. But it would not force poor people off the welfare roles.

There are other plans like the Boren-Simon proposal. One has been proposed by Mickey Kaus.

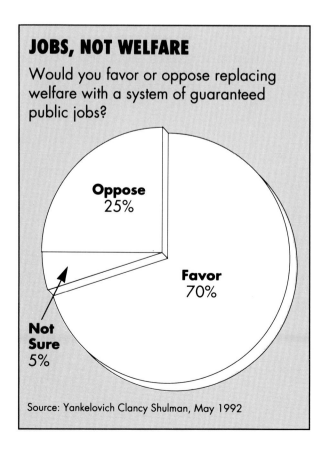

JOBS, NOT WELFARE

Would you favor or oppose replacing welfare with a system of guaranteed public jobs?

Oppose 25%

Favor 70%

Not Sure 5%

Source: Yankelovich Clancy Shulman, May 1992

Kaus is an editor of *The New Republic*. His plan would cut out all public aid to the able-bodied poor. Instead, public service jobs would be offered to anyone who wanted one. These jobs would be hard. They would pay a little less than minimum wage. That would encourage people to look for better jobs.

"Those who work in these jobs would earn their money," Kaus says. "They could hold their heads up." People would not have to work, of course. But if they did not, they would be on their own. "No cash doles," Kaus says. "Work would be all that is offered."

A 1992 poll showed that many Americans support this idea. Seven out of ten favored replacing the welfare system with a jobs program.

A Decent Wage

Jobs for everyone is the focus of Choice #4. But there is something else just as important, in this view. Those who work must be paid enough to live on. The U.S. has minimum wage laws, of course. But the minimum wage is not enough, people who favor this choice say. It does not provide a decent standard of living for working Americans.

It was different in the 1960s and 1970s. One full-time worker earning minimum wages was enough. It was enough to keep a family of three above the poverty line. The minimum wage was raised in 1991. It went from $3.35 an hour to $4.25 an hour. But now the pay of one full-time wage earner is not enough. It leaves a family of three 20% **below** the poverty line. That is one reason to raise the minimum wage, in this view.

There is another reason as well. Many people have to choose between welfare and a minimum wage job. In many cases, welfare is better. It pays more. It provides more benefits. It is not surprising that people do not want to work.

Many supporters of this view favor a

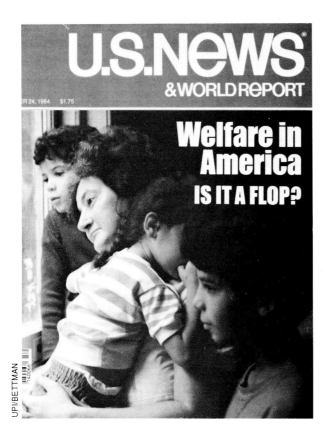

U.S. NEWS & WORLD REPORT

R 24, 1984 $1.75

Welfare in America IS IT A FLOP?

UPI/BETTMAN

minimum wage of $5.50. This would keep a family of three out of poverty. In this view, we should cut out cash benefits. But we should keep health and day care benefits. This would encourage people to take jobs that do not cover these needs.

Choice #4 would provide jobs for poor people. It would pay them enough to live on. It would give them a chance to make it on their own.

What Critics Say

Critics of this choice admit a jobs program is a good idea. But they say it will not work. And it will be too costly.

President Clinton says that this country needs to improve its public works. These include highways, roads, bridges, and railroads. He proposed adding $20 billion to the federal budget for these projects. But critics say that would hardly touch the jobless problem. Even spending twice that much would only reduce unemployment by 1%.

A public works program would have to give millions of Americans jobs. Each person would have to be paid minimum wage. That would cost taxpayers twice as much as the average aid payment.

The costs are just part of the problem, critics say. Many people on public aid are not prepared for work. They are poorly educated. They do not have good work habits. They do not feel they can do any job well. It would be very hard to supervise such workers.

Labor unions are not happy about offering public jobs to the poor. They are afraid it will displace workers who now have public jobs. They say this has happened before.

Many people also oppose raising the minimum wage. The point would be to encourage people to give up welfare. So, the minimum wage would have to be raised a lot. This would be too costly, they say.

Raising the minimum wage would also raise the cost of labor. Many employers could no longer afford to hire low-skill workers, critics say. So, there would be **fewer** jobs instead of more jobs.

This approach would cut off benefits for millions of poor people who do not work. That is the worst part of it, critics say. It would deny the right of the poor to public help. Jobs for the able-bodied poor may be part of the answer, says Rebecca Blank. "But it is not enough." She agrees that we must encourage people to work. But we cannot leave them and their children in poverty when employment fails.

Conclusion:
Decent Provision

There are three basic questions we should talk about. What do we owe the poor? What is the best kind of help to give? What do we have a right to expect in return?

Much of the poverty debate focuses on numbers and programs. We sometimes forget that we are talking about real people. We are talking about 35 million people living in poverty. They are people like Sean Hanan, who lost his job at Sears. He has not been able to find a job since then. We are talking about Tasha Barber, whose family has always been poor. She depends on AFDC and food stamps while she looks for a job.

The poor do not have much in common except one thing. They cannot make a living. President Franklin Roosevelt called them "the forgotten people." What do we owe the poor? How can we best help them? What can we expect them to do for themselves?

In the 1700s, England passed a set of Poor Laws. They were based on a view of how a humane society behaves. It does not let poor people starve in the streets. It makes what writer Samuel Johnson called "a decent provision" for the poor.

But deciding what that "decent provision" should be is not easy. Each of our choices answers the question in a different way. Each begins with a different view of the causes of poverty.

The Choices

People who favor **Choice #1** believe welfare programs are the **cause** of the problem. In this view,

NICULAE ASCIU

welfare payments have created a way of life. The system has made the poor depend on public help. The answer is to get rid of most welfare programs. That would force the poor to take care of themselves.

According to **Choice #2**, the poor are victims of our economic system. It is not their fault that they are poor. Society owes them a decent living.

Choice #3 is about what the poor owe in return for public help. In this view, poverty has become worse because welfare is a free ride. It does not encourage poor people to help themselves. Those who get benefits should be required to work if they can. They should be required to stay in school. And they should not have children they cannot support.

Choice #4 sees the lack of jobs as the main cause of poverty. In this view there is only one useful course of action. The government should ensure jobs for the able-bodied poor. And it should ensure decent wages for everyone who works.

What Do We Owe the Poor?

Some people think that the poor have a **right** to public aid. We owe them a "decent provision." But not everyone agrees with that view. They are not willing to spend their hard-earned money on strangers.

People opposed to aid programs do not see them as kindness. They believe such handouts hurt the poor in the long run. They believe public aid traps people in a cycle of poverty. It keeps them from behaving in ways that will help them stand on their own feet.

What course of action would be the kindest and most helpful? That is one question we should try to answer.

There is another question. How serious are we about wiping out poverty? How much are we willing to spend? We could make small changes in the welfare system. Many of these have been made in the past 30 years. But major reform of the system would be much harder. Some proposals, such as a public jobs programs, would be very costly.

Only we can answer these questions. We will have to decide what kind of society we want. We will have to talk about what should be done. That is what National Issues Forums are about.

For Further Reading

For general accounts of America's poverty problem, see Carl Chelf's *Controversial Issues in Social Welfare Policy* (Newbury Park, California: Sage Publications, 1992), which explores the role of government programs in alleviating poverty, hunger, homelessness and unemployment. *Fighting Poverty: What Works and What Doesn't*, edited by Sheldon Danziger and Daniel Weinberg (Cambridge, MA: Harvard University Press, 1986), reviews and assesses antipoverty efforts over the past several decades.

Christopher Jencks focuses on the underclass in *Rethinking Social Policy: Race, Poverty and the Underclass* (Cambridge, MA: Harvard University Press, 1992). Jencks is also co-editor, with Paul Peterson, of *The Urban Underclass* (Washington, D.C.: Brookings Institution, 1991).

For a comparison of the American system of providing for the poor with systems in Sweden, Britain, and Germany, see Norman Ginsburg's *Divisions of Welfare* (Newbury Park, CA: Sage Publications, 1992). For an analysis of the views of the American public, see *The Public's Perspective on Social Welfare Reform*, by John Doble and Keith Melville (New York: Public Agenda Foundation, 1988).

For a thoughtful account of American views on distributive justice, see Jennifer Hochschild's *What's Fair: American Beliefs about Distributive Justice* (Cambridge, MA: Harvard University Press, 1981).

The most comprehensive source of information about the American welfare program is the *Green Book: Overview of Entitlement Programs* published annually by the Committee on Ways and Means of the House of Representatives (Washington, D.C.: Government Printing Office).

From the perspective of the first choice, see Charles Murray's *Losing Ground* (New York: Basic Books, 1984); George Gilder's *Wealth and Poverty* (New York: Basic Books, 1981); Marvin Olasky's *The Tragedy of American Compassion* (Lanham, MD: Regnery Gateway, 1992); a chapter by Robert Rector and Mike McLaughlin entitled "A Conservative's Guide to State Level Welfare Reform," in *Conservative Agenda for the States* (Austin: Texas Public Policy Foundation, 1992); and Stuart Butler and Anna Kondratas' *Out of the Poverty Trap: A Conservative Strategy for Welfare Reform* (New York: Free Press, 1987).

For critiques of the conservative view, see Robert Greenstein's article, "Losing Faith in 'Losing Ground,'" which appeared in *The New Republic*, March 25, 1985. See also *The Mean Season: The Attack on the Welfare State*, by Fred Block, Richard A. Cloward, Barbara Ehrenreich, and Frances Fox Piven (New York: Pantheon, 1987).

From the perspective of the second choice, see *Uneven Tides: Rising Inequality in the 1980s* edited by Sheldon Danziger and Peter Gottschalk (New York: Russell Sage Foundation Press, 1992), Theodore Marmor, Jerry Mashaw, and Philip Harvey's book, *America's Misunderstood Welfare State* (New York: Basic Books, 1990);

Michael Katz's *The Undeserving Poor* (New York: Pantheon, 1989); *Economic Justice for All*, a report from the National Conference of Catholic Bishops (Washington, D.C.: 1986), and *The Common Good*, a report prepared by the Ford Foundation Project on Social Welfare and the American Future (New York: 1989).

From the perspective of the third choice, see two titles by Lawrence Mead: *Beyond Entitlement* (New York: Free Press, 1986) and *The New Politics of Poverty: The Nonworking Poor in America* (New York: Basic Books, 1992). Robert Rector writes about requiring work and other responsible behavior in return for benefits in "Strategies for Welfare Reform," (Washington, D.C.: Heritage Foundation, 1992). For various examples of this strategy, see an article by Julie Kosterlitz entitled "Behavior Modification," which appeared in *National Journal*, February 1, 1992. See also Isabel Sawhill's article, "The New Paternalism: Earned Welfare," which appeared in the Spring 1992 issue of *The Responsive Community*.

From the perspective of the fourth choice, see John E. Schwarz and Thomas Volgy's *The Forgotten Americans: Thirty Million Working Poor in the Land of Opportunity* (New York: Norton, 1992), and Mickey Kaus' *The End of Equality* (New York: Basic Books, 1992). See also David Ellwood's *Poor Support* (New York: Basic Books, 1988). For a summary of initiatives that help welfare recipients become self-sufficient, see Judith Gueron and Edward Pauly's, *From Welfare to Work* (New York: Russell Sage Foundation, 1991).

Acknowledgments

We would like to express our appreciation to the people who helped choose this year's topics and took part in discussions about how they should be approached. Once again, David Mathews and Daniel Yankelovich provided both guidance and support. Our colleagues Jean Johnson, Jon Rye Kinghorn, Robert Kingston, Patrick Scully, and Deborah Wadsworth played a valuable role in refining the framework and clarifying the presentation.

Special thanks to the individuals who helped us as consultants and reviewers, including Robert Greenstein, Isaac Shapiro, and Susan Steinmetz at the Center on Budget and Policy Priorities; Lawrence Mead, and Robert Rector.

What Are National Issues Forums?

The National Issues Forums bring people together to talk about important issues. These Forums are held each fall, winter, and spring. They are held in communities across the U.S. The results of the Forums are shared with local and national government leaders. Thousands of different groups sponsor the Forums. Each group handles the Forums in its own way. No two are exactly alike. Here are some of the questions people ask about the Forums:

"What happens in Forums?"

The goal of the Forums is to consider a special issue. The issues are very complicated —like health care, crime, and the economy. There are many ways to look at each issue. People have different ideas about how to solve the problem. In the Forums, ideas are shared. We call this "choice work." Choice means we have considered all points of view and what will happen if one choice or point of view is chosen. Each person must think as an individual but also as part of a community.

"What if I don't know much about the issue?"

To consider an issue, a person needs some information about the topic but no one needs to be an expert. It is more important to be able to listen and share ideas. This means looking into the values behind the facts. It means thinking about what the future will be like if we make a certain choice. Policymaking is not just for experts. It requires the public's common sense.

"What's the point of one more bull session?"

In a Forum, we do much more than talk about the topic. The work of the Forum is to understand choices. The different plans that are discussed will all have good and bad points. In a Forum, we must look at the consequences of choices. This means we "work through" an issue — not just "talk about" an issue.

"Isn't my opinion as good as another's?"

Yes, each person's opinion is as good as another's. But remember, the work of the Forum is to understand choices. This means making judgments. Groups usually make better judgments than individuals. This happens because of the sharing and studying of different ideas.

"Are we expected to agree on one choice?"

No, each group is not expected to agree on one choice. It is more important for the group to be able to see the good and bad in all choices. In real life, choices are seldom easy. Often, we do not find a perfect answer to problems. We often have to choose a plan we can "live with."

"Do the Forums lead to any action?"

The results of the Forums and ballots are shared with government leaders. The National Issues Forums do not suggest one choice or plan to the leaders. Instead, they share how the people feel about a topic. This information can help leaders plan future action.

Pre-Forum Ballot
The Poverty Puzzle:
What Should Be Done to Help the Poor?

People get involved in National Issues Forums partly because they want leaders to know how they feel about the issues. Each year, NIF reports what you say to local and national leaders. Please answer the questions below BEFORE you read this book. But before answering the questions, make up a three-digit number. Fill in your three-digit number here. ☐☐☐

When you have answered the questions, please give this form to your Forum leader. Or mail it to National Issues Forums, 100 Commons Road, Dayton, Ohio 45459-2777.

---

1. Here are four views about why we still have poverty in the U.S. How important do you think each one is? Give the most important reason a 1. Give the next most important a 2. Give the third most important a 3. Give the least important a 4.

We still have poverty in the U.S. because:

   _____ a. Welfare programs give people who are able to work less reason to look for jobs and help themselves.

   _____ b. There are basic problems in our free market system that make some people poor through no fault of their own.

   _____ c. Many welfare programs give help unconditionally without requiring people to take steps to improve their own lives.

   _____ d. We have fewer and fewer factory jobs that would enable poor people to earn a decent living.

---

2. How do you feel about each of these approaches to reducing poverty in the U.S?

	Favor	Oppose	Not Sure
a. We should severely **cut back** on welfare to force people to make it on their own, **EVEN IF** this would be very hard on some of the poor for a while.	☐	☐	☐
b. We should **increase** government help to the poor, **EVEN IF** this means cutting back on other public programs.	☐	☐	☐
c. We should require people on welfare to get job training or finish high school, **EVEN IF** this means government interfering in people's private lives.	☐	☐	☐
d. The government should create millions of new public service jobs, **EVEN IF** the cost of this would raise taxes.	☐	☐	☐

2A. Look again at the approaches you **opposed** in Question 2. Are there any you could live with if other people favored those approaches? If so, which one(s)?

☐ a.   ☐ b.   ☐ c.   ☐ d.

(over)

3. Here are some views people have about each choice. How do you feel about them?

	Agree	Disagree	Not Sure
Choice #1: The Welfare Trap			
a. The growing number of poor people proves that welfare programs have not worked.	☐	☐	☐
b. Reducing welfare would cause suffering for poor children and others who cannot help themselves.	☐	☐	☐
c. Businesses that create new jobs in poor areas should get tax breaks.	☐	☐	☐
Choice #2: The Rights of the Poor			
a. Other prosperous nations guarantee a basic standard of living to their citizens, and so should we.	☐	☐	☐
b. Increasing welfare benefits would encourage people who could work to stay on welfare.	☐	☐	☐
c. We should increase government benefits enough to meet everyone's basic living needs.	☐	☐	☐
Choice #3: A New Compact with the Poor			
a. Making people on welfare go to school or get training will keep them out of poverty in the long run.	☐	☐	☐
b. Making people do something in exchange for welfare would give government too much power over people's lives.	☐	☐	☐
c. We should require able-bodied people on welfare to work in community service jobs in exchange for their benefits.	☐	☐	☐
Choice #4: Jobs Strategy			
a. The best way to get people off welfare is to have enough jobs for them.	☐	☐	☐
b. Considering the size of the budget deficit, it would be too costly to give millions of poor people public jobs.	☐	☐	☐
c. We should raise the minimum wage so that Americans working full-time will not be poor.	☐	☐	☐

---

4. Which of these age groups are you in?   ☐ Under 18   ☐ 18 to 29   ☐ 30 to 44   ☐ 45 to 64   ☐ over 64

---

5. Are you a: ☐ Man   ☐ Woman

---

6. Do you consider yourself: ☐ White   ☐ Black or African-American   ☐ Hispanic
☐ Asian   ☐ Other (Specify:_____)

---

7. Have you completed: ☐ Grade school or less   ☐ Some high school   ☐ High school
☐ Vocational/technical school   ☐ Some college   ☐ College   ☐ Postgraduate work

---

8. Do you live in the: ☐ Northeast   ☐ South   ☐ Midwest   ☐ West   ☐ Southwest

---

9. What is your ZIP CODE?_____

Post-Forum Ballot
The Poverty Puzzle:
What Should Be Done to Help the Poor?

People get involved in National Issues Forums partly because they want leaders to know how they feel about the issues. Each year, NIF reports what you say to local and national leaders. Please answer the questions below AFTER you read this book. Fill in the same three-digit number here.

When you have answered the questions, please give this form to your Forum leader. Or mail it to National Issues Forums, 100 Commons Road, Dayton, Ohio 45459-2777.

1. Here are four views about why we still have poverty in the U.S. How important do you think each one is? Give the most important reason a 1. Give the next most important a 2. Give the third most important a 3. Give the least important a 4.

We still have poverty in the U.S. because:

   ____   a.   Welfare programs give people who are able to work less reason to look for jobs and help themselves.

   ____   b.   There are basic problems in our free market system that make some people poor through no fault of their own.

   ____   c.   Many welfare programs give help unconditionally without requiring people to take steps to improve their own lives.

   ____   d.   We have fewer and fewer factory jobs that would enable poor people to earn a decent living.

2. How do you feel about each of these approaches to reducing poverty in the U.S?

	Favor	Oppose	Not Sure
a. We should severely **cut back** on welfare to force people to make it on their own, **EVEN IF** this would be very hard on some of the poor for a while.	☐	☐	☐
b. We should **increase** government help to the poor, **EVEN IF** this means cutting back on other public programs.	☐	☐	☐
c. We should require people on welfare to get job training or finish high school, **EVEN IF** this means government interfering in people's private lives.	☐	☐	☐
d. The government should create millions of new public service jobs, **EVEN IF** the cost of this would raise taxes.	☐	☐	☐

2A. Look again at the approaches you **opposed** in Question 2. Are there any you could live with if other people favored those approaches? If so, which one(s)?

☐ a.   ☐ b.   ☐ c.   ☐ d.

(over)

3. Here are some views people have about each choice. How do you feel about them?

		Agree	Disagree	Not Sure
Choice #1: The Welfare Trap				
a.	The growing number of poor people proves that welfare programs have not worked.	☐	☐	☐
b.	Reducing welfare would cause suffering for poor children and others who cannot help themselves.	☐	☐	☐
c.	Businesses that create new jobs in poor areas should get tax breaks.	☐	☐	☐
Choice #2: The Rights of the Poor				
a.	Other prosperous nations guarantee a basic standard of living to their citizens, and so should we.	☐	☐	☐
b.	Increasing welfare benefits would encourage people who could work to stay on welfare.	☐	☐	☐
c.	We should increase government benefits enough to meet everyone's basic living needs.	☐	☐	☐
Choice #3: A New Compact with the Poor				
a.	Making people on welfare go to school or get training will keep them out of poverty in the long run.	☐	☐	☐
b.	Making people do something in exchange for welfare would give government too much power over people's lives.	☐	☐	☐
c.	We should require able-bodied people on welfare to work in community service jobs in exchange for their benefits.	☐	☐	☐
Choice #4: Jobs Strategy				
a.	The best way to get people off welfare is to have enough jobs for them.	☐	☐	☐
b.	Considering the size of the budget deficit, it would be too costly to give millions of poor people public jobs.	☐	☐	☐
c.	We should raise the minimum wage so that Americans working full-time will not be poor.	☐	☐	☐

---

4. Now that you have talked about poverty in the U.S., has your understanding of this issue:

☐ increased a lot   ☐ increased a little   ☐ not increased at all   ☐ not sure

4A. If your understanding has increased at all, in what ways has it increased?

---

5. Has your understanding of **other people's** views on this issue:

☐ increased a lot   ☐ increased a little   ☐ not increased at all   ☐ not sure

5A. If your understanding of **other people's** views has increased at all, in what ways has it increased?

---

6. What is your ZIP CODE?_____